INSIGHTS
Love

INSIGHTS
Love

What the Bible Tells Us about Christian Love

WILLIAM BARCLAY

SAINT ANDREW PRESS
Edinburgh

First published in 2012 by
SAINT ANDREW PRESS
121 George Street
Edinburgh EH2 4YN

ISBN 978 0 7152 0960 8

British Library Cataloguing in Publication Date
A catalogue record for this book is available from the British Library.

It is the publisher's policy to only use papers that are natural and
recyclable and that have been manufactured from timber grown
in renewable, properly managed forests. All of the manufacturing
processes of the papers are expected to conform to the environmental
regulations of the country of origin.

Typeset by Waverley Typesetters, Warham, Norfolk
Printed and bound by CPI Group (UK), Croydon

Contents

Foreword

Scholar, teacher, preacher and pastor, William Barclay made complex ideas simple and new thoughts familiar. This book contains a selection of his writings about love. Thirty, forty, even fifty years after he wrote them his words are as fresh as ever: they still illustrate how clearly he thought, and they demonstrate what a widely read scholar he was. This book communicates especially well, however, because its topic was so dear to his heart. The Love of God was the key to Barclay's understanding of the gospel of Jesus.

I will never forget hearing William Barclay speak on the radio about one of the miracles of Jesus – the stilling of the storm. Jesus and his disciples were in the boat. The disciples, terrified at the rising waves, wakened Jesus who was asleep on a pillow. In answer to their fears Jesus said to the wind and waves 'Be still', and the wind dropped and the sea was calm. Barclay was speaking of this miracle as he told the story of the tragic loss of his daughter in a sailing accident when she was only nineteen. 'God did not still the storm that took my daughter's life,' he said finally, 'but he stilled the storm in me.' What was the conviction which could enable a grieving father so humbly to accept the loss of his daughter? Even such bereavement did not wipe out his belief in the love of God. From the day that I heard that broadcast I listened to

Barclay and I read his books with a sense that here was a faith to live by.

In these fifteen reflections Barclay sets before his reader the results of his scholarship and his meditation. Each one explores a passage of the New Testament – some from the Gospels, others from the letters of Paul and John. Barclay the scholar explains the history of the text; Barclay the teacher draws on the thoughts of others who have studied the issues in earlier times; and Barclay the pastor encourages the reader to explore the true meaning of living in the light of the love of God.

In my own working life as a church minister I have seen time and again the astonishing effect of love. I have seen mothers devoting themselves to the endless needs of their children, wives caring for dying husbands, husbands for dying wives; neighbours looking after neighbours as if they were family; selfless kindness shown to ungrateful individuals. And I have seen people who hated themselves confronted with the transforming thought that they, even they, were loved by God.

William Barclay's consideration of such experiences as these led him to a profound conclusion. Barclay believed that the love of God would not leave anyone out. He was what theologians call 'a universalist'. In his *Spiritual Autobiography* he wrote, 'I am a convinced universalist. I believe that in the end all men will be gathered into the love of God.'[1] Because of what he read in the Bible and the picture it gave him of the way God looks at the world, Barclay believed that absolutely

---

[1]   William Barclay, *A Spiritual Autobiography*, William B. Eerdmans Publishing Company, Grand Rapids, Michigan, 1977, p. 65.

everyone, no matter how darkened by evil they may have been, will at the end be enfolded in the love of God. This estimate of the unfailing energy of the gift of love is present throughout this selection of Barclay's writing on Love.

Although I never met William Barclay, I heard that his house was not far from where I lived. Sometimes I would make a short detour to pass his house, and as I went past I could occasionally see him seated at a desk in a ground-floor window, typing out the material for whatever was to be his next book. To read his crisp, clear, uncompromising, compassionate words in this book is to have him brought vividly again to my mind. This book is issued in the hope that a new generation of enquirers and believers will be enriched by Barclay's unique writings.

JOHN MILLER

Publisher's Introduction

In what is possibly the most famous verse in the whole New Testament (John 3:16), we are told that God loved the world so much that he 'gave his only Son' so that we might have life. Love is at the heart of the New Testament message – God's love for the world, Jesus' love for all with whom he came into contact and his final commandment that we should love one another in that same way.

William Barclay takes us through these various instructions about love, explaining the different nuances of the words used for 'love' in the Greek language. He shows us how Jesus expanded the Jewish commandment to love God and neighbour not only by presenting a new perspective on exactly who that neighbour might be – in the parable of the Good Samaritan – but also in the startling statement that we must love our enemies as well.

We learn that the parable of the Prodigal Son is really a story about a father's love and, in the story of about Jesus' anointing at the house of his friends Lazarus, Martha and Mary at Bethany, that love requires complete, unselfconscious and humble giving. In an extended discussion of St Paul's famous 'hymn to love' in his first letter to the Corinthians Barclay presents Christian love as the greatest of all spiritual gifts, a gift that was made real in the life of Jesus himself.

Such love is permanent and complete, it is 'the fire which give the spark to faith, and it is the light which turns hope into certainty'.

The examples of teaching about love found here in *Insights: Love* all have a wider context, which you can find in Barclay's *New Daily Study Bible* series. Each book of the New Testament has its own writer, style of writing, historical background, original readership and so on. In reading about these, we can add to our understanding of the Bible. We hope you will be inspired to learn more about the New Testament through William Barclay's classic books. A list of them can be found at the end of this book.

The love of God

John 3:16

> 'For God so loved the world that he gave his only Son so that everyone who believes in him should not perish but have everlasting life.'

ALL great men and women have had their favourite texts, but this has been called 'everybody's text'. Herein for every one of us is the very essence of the gospel. This text tells us certain great things.

(1) It tells us that the initiative in all salvation lies with God. Sometimes Christianity is presented in such a way that it sounds as if God had to be pacified, as if he had to be persuaded to forgive. Sometimes the picture is drawn of a stern, angry, unforgiving God and a gentle, loving, forgiving Jesus. Sometimes the Christian message is presented in such a way that it sounds as if Jesus did something which changed the attitude of God to men and women from condemnation to forgiveness. But this text tells us that it was with God that it all started. It was God who sent his Son, and he sent him because he loved the world he had created. At the back of everything is the love of God.

(2) It tells us that the mainspring of God's being is love. It is easy to think of God as looking at human beings in their heedlessness and their disobedience and their rebellion and saying: 'I'll break them: I'll discipline them and punish them and scourge them until they come back.' It is easy to think of

1

God as seeking human allegiance in order to satisfy his own desire for power and for what we might call a completely subject universe. The tremendous thing about this text is that it shows us God acting not for his own sake but for ours; not to satisfy his desire for power, not to bring a universe to heel, but to satisfy his love. God is not like an absolute monarch who treats each individual as a subject to be reduced to abject obedience. God is the Father who cannot be happy until his wandering children have come home. God does not smash people into submission; he yearns over them and woos them into love.

(3) It tells us of the width of the love of God. It was *the world* that God so loved. It was not a nation; it was not the good people; it was not only the people who loved him; it was the world. The unlovable and the unlovely, the lonely who have no one else to love them, those who love God and those who never think of him, those who rest in the love of God and those who spurn it – all are included in this vast inclusive love of God. As St Augustine had it: 'God loves each one of us as if there was only one of us to love.'

Love for God and love for neighbour

Mark 12:28–34

> One of the experts in the law, who had listened to the
> discussion, and who realized that Jesus had answered them
> well, approached him and asked him, 'What is the first
> commandment of all?' Jesus answered, '"The Lord thy God
> is one Lord, and you must love the Lord your God with your
> whole heart, and your whole soul, and your whole mind,
> and your whole strength." This is the second, "You must love
> your neighbour as yourself." There is no other commandment
> which is greater than these.' The expert in the law said to him,
> 'Teacher, you have in truth spoken well, because God is one,
> and there is no other except him, and to love him with your
> whole heart, and your whole understanding, and your whole
> strength, and to love your neighbour as yourself is better than
> all burnt offerings of whole victims and sacrifices.' When Jesus
> saw that he had answered wisely, he said to him, 'You are not
> far from the kingdom of God.' And no one any longer dared
> to ask him any questions.

No love was lost between the expert in the law and the
Sadducees. The profession of the scribes was to interpret the
law in all its many rules and regulations. Their trade was to
know and to apply the oral law, while, as we have seen, the
Sadducees did not accept the oral law at all. The expert in the
law would no doubt be well satisfied with the discomfiture
of the Sadducees.

3

This scribe came to Jesus with a question which was often a matter of debate in the Rabbinic schools. In Judaism there was a kind of double tendency. There was the tendency to expand the law limitlessly into hundreds and thousands of rules and regulations. But there was also the tendency to try to gather up the law into one sentence, one general statement which would be a compendium of its whole message. Rabbi Hillel was once asked by a proselyte, a convert to Judaism, to instruct him in the whole law while he stood on one leg. Hillel's answer was, 'What thou hatest for thyself, do not to thy neighbour. This is the whole law, the rest is commentary. Go and learn.' Rabbi Akiba had already said, '"Thou shalt love thy neighbour as thyself" – this is the greatest general principle in the law.' Simon the Righteous had said, 'On three things stands the world – on the law, on the worship, and on works of love.'

Sammlai had taught that Moses received 613 precepts on Mount Sinai, 365 according to the days of the sun year, and 248 according to the generations. David reduced the 613 to 11 in Psalm 15.

> *O Lord, who may abide in your tent? Who may dwell on your holy hill?*
> 1. *Those who walk blamelessly.*
> 2. *And do what is right.*
> 3. *And speak truth from their hearts.*
> 4. *Who do not slander with their tongues.*
> 5. *And do no evil to their friends.*
> 6. *Nor take up a reproach against their neighbours.*
> 7. *In whose eyes the wicked are despised.*
> 8. *But who honour those who fear the Lord.*
> 9. *Who stand by their oath even to their hurt.*

10. *Who do not lend money at interest.*
11. *And do not take a bribe against the innocent.*

Isaiah reduced them to six (Isaiah 33:15).

1. *Those who walk righteously.*
2. *And speak uprightly.*
3. *Who despise the gain of oppressions.*
4. *Who wave away a bribe instead of accepting it.*
5. *Who stop their ears from hearing of bloodshed.*
6. *And shut their eyes from looking on evil.*

They will live on the heights.

Micah reduced the six to three (Micah 6:8).

He has told you, O mortal, what is good; and what does the Lord require of you?

1. *To do justice.*
2. *To love kindness.*
3. *To walk humbly with your God.*

Once again Isaiah brought the three down to two (Isaiah 56:1).

1. *Maintain justice.*
2. *Do what is right.*

Finally Habakkuk reduced them all to one (Habakkuk 2:4).

The righteous live by their faith.

It can be seen that Rabbinic ingenuity did try to contract as well as to expand the law. There were really two schools of thought. There were those who believed that there were lighter and weightier matters of the law, that there were great principles which were all important to grasp. As Augustine later said, 'Love God – and do what you like.' But there were others who were much against this, who held that every smallest principle was equally binding and that to try to distinguish between their relative importance was highly dangerous. The expert who asked Jesus this question was asking about something which was a living issue in Jewish thought and discussion.

For answer Jesus took two great commandments and put them together.

(1) 'Hear, O Israel: The Lord is our God, the Lord alone.' That single sentence is the real creed of Judaism (Deuteronomy 6:4). It had three uses. It is called *the Shema*. *Shema* is the imperative of the Hebrew verb *to hear*, and it is so called from the first word in the sentence.

(a) It was the sentence with which the service of the synagogue always began and still begins. The full Shema is Deuteronomy 6:4–9, 11:13–21; Numbers 15:37–41. It is the declaration that God is the only God, the foundation of Jewish monotheism.

(b) The three passages of the Shema were contained in the *phylacteries* (Matthew 23:5), little leather boxes which devout Jews wore on their foreheads and on their wrists when they were at prayer. As they prayed they reminded themselves of their creed. The warrant for wearing *phylacteries* is found in Deuteronomy 6:8.

(c) The Shema was contained in a little cylindrical box called the *Mezuzah*, which was and still is affixed to the door of every Jewish house and the door of every room within it, to remind Jewish families of God as they went out and as they came in.

When Jesus quoted this sentence as the first command-ment, every devout Jew would agree with him.

(2) 'You shall love your neighbour as yourself.' That is a quotation from Leviticus 19:18. Jesus did one thing with it. In its original context it has to do only with *fellow Jews*. It would not have included the Gentiles, whom it was quite permissible to hate. But Jesus quoted it without qualification and without limiting boundaries. He took an old law and filled it with a new meaning.

The new thing that Jesus did was to put these two com-mandments together. No Rabbi had ever done that before. There is only one suggestion of connection previously. Round about 100 BC there was composed a series of tractates called The Testaments of the Twelve Patriarchs, in which an unknown writer put into the mouths of the patriarchs some very fine teaching. In the Testament of Issachar (5:2), we read:

> Love the Lord and love your neighbour,
> Have compassion on the poor and weak.

In the same testament (7:6), we read:

> I loved the Lord,
> Likewise also every man with my whole heart.

In the Testament of Dan (5:3), we read:

> Love the Lord through all your life,
> And one another with a true heart.

But no one until Jesus put the two commandments together and made them one. Religion to him was loving God and loving one another. He would have said that the only way to prove love for God is by showing love for others.

The scribe willingly accepted this, and went on to say that such a love was better than all sacrifices. In that, he was in line with the highest thought of his people. Long, long ago Samuel had said, 'Has the Lord as great delight in burnt offerings and sacrifices, as in obedience to the voice of the Lord? Surely, to obey is better than sacrifice, and to heed than the fat of rams' (1 Samuel 15:22). Hosea had heard God say, 'I desire steadfast love and not sacrifice' (Hosea 6:6).

But it is always easy to let ritual take the place of love. It is always easy to let worship become a matter of the church building instead of a matter of the whole life. The priest and the Levite could pass by the wounded traveller because they were eager to get on with the ritual of the Temple. This scribe had risen beyond his contemporaries, and that is why he found himself in sympathy with Jesus.

There must have been a look of love in Jesus' eyes, and a look of appeal as he said to him, 'You have gone so far. Will you not come further and accept my way of things? Then you will be a true citizen of the kingdom.'

Who is my neighbour?

Luke 10:25–37

Look you – an expert in the law stood up and asked Jesus a test question. 'Teacher,' he said, 'what is it I am to do to become the possessor of eternal life?' He said to him, 'What stands written in the law? How do you read?' He answered, 'You must love the Lord your God with your whole heart, and with your whole mind, and your neighbour as yourself.' 'Your answer is correct,' said Jesus. But he, wishing to put himself in the right, said to Jesus, 'And who is my neighbour?' Jesus answered, 'There was a man who went down from Jerusalem to Jericho. He fell among brigands who stripped him and laid blows upon him, and went away and left him half-dead. Now, by chance, a priest came down by that road. He looked at him and passed by on the other side. In the same way when a Levite came to the place he looked at him and passed by on the other side. A Samaritan who was on the road came to where he was. He looked at him and was moved to the depths of his being with pity. So he came up to him and bound up his wounds, pouring in wine and oil; and he put him on his own beast and brought him to an inn and cared for him. On the next day he put down two denarii and gave it to the innkeeper. "Look after him," he said, "and whatever more you are out of pocket, when I come back this way, I'll square up with you in full." Which of these three, do you think, was neighbour to the man who fell into the hands of brigands?' He said, 'He who showed mercy on him.' 'Go,' said Jesus to him, 'and do likewise.'

First, let us look at *the scene* of this story. The road from Jerusalem to Jericho was a notoriously dangerous road. Jerusalem is 2,300 feet above sea level; the Dead Sea, near which Jericho stood, is 1,300 feet below sea level. So then, in somewhat less than twenty miles, this road dropped 3,600 feet. It was a road of narrow, rocky passages, and of sudden turnings which made it the happy hunting-ground of brigands. In the fifth century Jerome tells us that it was still called 'The Red, or Bloody Way'. In the nineteenth century it was still necessary to pay safety money to the local Sheiks before one could travel on it. As late as the early 1930s the travel writer H. V. Morton tells us that he was warned to get home before dark, if he intended to use the road, because a certain Abu Jildah was an adept at holding up cars and robbing travellers and tourists, and escaping to the hills before the police could arrive. When Jesus told this story, he was telling about the kind of thing that was constantly happening on the Jerusalem to Jericho road.

Second, let us look at the *characters*.

(a) There was *the traveller*. He was obviously a reckless and foolhardy character. People seldom attempted the Jerusalem to Jericho road alone if they were carrying goods or valuables. Seeking safety in numbers, they travelled in convoys or caravans. This man had no one but himself to blame for the plight in which he found himself.

(b) There was *the priest*. He hastened past. No doubt he was remembering that anyone who touched a dead man was unclean for seven days (Numbers 19:11). He could not be sure but he feared that the man was dead; to touch him would mean losing his turn of duty in the Temple; and he refused to risk that. He set the claims of ceremonial above those of charity. The Temple and its liturgy meant more to him than human suffering.

(c) There was *the Levite*. He seems to have gone nearer to the man before he passed on. The bandits were in the habit of using decoys. One of their number would act the part of a wounded man; and when some unsuspecting traveller stopped over him, the others would rush upon him and overpower him. The Levite was a man whose motto was, 'Safety first'. He would take no risks to help anyone else.

(d) There was *the Samaritan*. The listeners would obviously expect that with his arrival the villain had arrived. He may not have been *racially* a Samaritan at all. The Jews had no dealings with the Samaritans and yet this man seems to have been a kind of commercial traveller who was a regular visitor to the inn. In John 8:48 the Jews call Jesus a Samaritan. The name was sometimes used to describe someone who was considered a heretic and a breaker of the ceremonial law. Perhaps this man was a Samaritan in the sense of being one whom orthodox good people despised.

We note two things about him.

(1) His credit was good! Clearly the innkeeper was prepared to trust him. He may have been theologically unsound, but he was an honest man.

(2) He alone was prepared to help. A heretic he may have been, but the love of God was in his heart. It is not uncommon to find the orthodox more interested in dogmas than in help and to find those whom the orthodox despise to be the ones who show the greatest love for others. In the end we will be judged not by the creed we hold but by the life we live.

Third, let us look at *the teaching* of the parable. The scribe who asked this question was in earnest. Jesus asked him what was written in the law, and then said, 'How do you read?' Strict orthodox Jews wore round their wrists little leather boxes called phylacteries, which contained certain passages of Scripture – Exodus 13:1–10, 11–16; Deuteronomy 6:4–9, 11:13–20. 'You shall love the Lord your God' is from Deuteronomy 6:4 and 11:13. So Jesus said to the scribe, 'Look at the phylactery on your own wrist and it will answer your question.' To that the scribes added Leviticus 19:18, which has the bidding 'love your neighbour as yourself'; but with their passion for definition the Rabbis sought to define who a person's neighbour was; and at their worst and their narrowest they confined the word *neighbour* to their *fellow Jews*. For instance, some of them said that it was illegal to help a Gentile woman in her sorest time, the time of childbirth, for that would only have been to bring another Gentile into the world. So then the scribe's question, 'Who is my neighbour?' was genuine.

Jesus' answer involves three things.

(1) We must be prepared to help others even when they have brought their trouble on themselves, as the traveller had done.

(2) Anyone from any nation who is in need is our neighbour. Our help must be as wide as the love of God.

(3) The help must be practical and not consist merely in *feeling* sorry. No doubt the priest and the Levite felt a pang of pity for the wounded man, but they *did* nothing. Compassion, to be real, must issue in deeds.

What Jesus said to the scribe, he says to us – 'Go *you* and do the same.'

Christian love

Matthew 5:43–8

'You have heard that it has been said, "You shall love your neighbour, and you shall hate your enemy"; but I say to you: Love your enemies, and pray for those who persecute you, so that you may become the sons of your Father who is in heaven; for he makes his sun to rise on the evil and the good, and sends rain on the righteous and the unrighteous. If you love those who love you, what reward can you expect? Do not even the tax-gatherers do that? If you greet only your brothers, where is there anything extra about that? Do not even the Gentiles do that? So, then, you must be perfect even as your heavenly Father is perfect.'

1. The meaning of it

C. G. MONTEFIORE, the Jewish scholar, calls this 'the central and most famous section' of the Sermon on the Mount. It is certainly true that there is no other passage of the New Testament which contains such a concentrated expression of the Christian ethic of personal relations. To the ordinary person, this passage describes essential Christianity in action, and even the person who never darkens the door of the church knows that Jesus said this, and very often condemns the professing Christian for falling so far short of its demands.

When we study this passage, we must first try to find out what Jesus was really saying and what he was demanding of his followers. If we are to try to live this out, we must obviously first of all be quite clear as to what it is asking. What does Jesus mean by *loving our enemies*?

Greek is a language which is rich in synonyms; its words often have shades of meaning which English does not possess. In Greek, there are four different words for *love*.

(1) There is the noun *storgē* with its accompanying verb *stergein*. These words are the characteristic words of *family love*. They are the words which describe the love of a parent for a child and a child for a parent. 'A child', said Plato, '*loves* [*stergein*] and is loved by those who brought him into the world.' 'Sweet is a father to his children,' said Philemon, 'if he has *love* [*storgē*].' These words describe family affection.

(2) There is the noun *erōs* and the accompanying verb *eran*. These words describe the love between the sexes; there is always passion there; and there is always sexual love. Sophocles described *erōs* as 'the terrible longing'. In these words, there is nothing essentially bad; they simply describe the passion of human love; but as time went on, they began to be tinged with the idea of lust rather than love, and they never occur in the New Testament at all.

(3) There is *philia* with its accompanying verb *philein*. These are the warmest and the best Greek words for love. They describe real love, real affection. *Ho philountes*, the present participle, is the word which describes a person's closest and nearest and truest friends. It is the word which is used in the famous saying of the Greek poet Menander: 'Whom the gods *love*, dies young.' *Philein* can mean to *caress* or to *kiss*. It is the word of warm, tender affection, the highest kind of love.

(4) There is *agapē* with its accompanying verb *agapan*. These words indicate *unconquerable benevolence*, *invincible*

goodwill. (*Agapē* is the word which is used here.) If we regard people with *agapē*, it means that no matter what they do to us, no matter how they treat us, no matter if they insult us or injure us or grieve us, we will never allow any bitterness against them to invade our hearts, but will regard them with that unconquerable benevolence and goodwill which will seek nothing but their highest good. From this, certain things emerge.

(1) Jesus never asked us to love our enemies in the same way as we love our nearest and dearest. The very word is different; to love our enemies in the same way as we love our nearest and dearest would be neither possible nor right. This is a different kind of love.

(2) Wherein does the main difference lie? In the case of our nearest and dearest, we cannot help loving them; we speak of *falling in love*; it is something which comes to us quite unsought; it is something which is born of the emotions of the heart. But in the case of our enemies, love is not only something of the *heart*; it is also something of the *will*. It is not something which we cannot help; it is something which we have to will ourselves into doing. It is in fact a victory over that which comes instinctively to us by our very nature.

Agapē does not mean a feeling of the heart, which we cannot help, and which comes unbidden and unsought; it means a determination of the mind, whereby we achieve this unconquerable goodwill even to those who hurt and injure us. *Agapē*, someone has said, is the power to love those whom we do not like and who may not like us. In point of fact, we can only have *agapē* when Jesus Christ enables us to conquer our natural tendency to anger and to bitterness, and to achieve this invincible goodwill to all people.

(3) It is then quite obvious that the last thing *agapē*, Christian love, means is that we allow people to do absolutely as they like, and that we leave them quite unchecked. No one would say that parents really love their children if they let them do as they like. If we regard people with invincible goodwill, it will often mean that we must punish them, that we must restrain them, that we must discipline them, that we must protect them against themselves. But it will also mean that we do not punish them to satisfy our desire for revenge, but in order to make them better people. It will always mean that all Christian discipline and all Christian punishment must be aimed not at vengeance but at cure. Punishment will never be merely retributive; it will always be remedial.

(4) It must be noted that Jesus laid this love down as a basis for *personal relationships*. People use this passage as a basis for pacifism and as a text on which to speak about international relationships. Of course, it includes that, but first and foremost it deals with our personal relationships with our family and our neighbours and the people we meet with every day in life. It is very much easier to go about declaring that there should be no such thing as war between nation and nation, than to live a life in which we personally never allow any such thing as bitterness to invade our relationships with those we meet with every day. First and foremost, this commandment of Jesus deals with personal relationships. It is a commandment of which we should say first and foremost: 'This means me.'

(5) We must note that this commandment is possible only for a Christian. Only the grace of Jesus Christ can enable us to have this unconquerable benevolence and this invincible goodwill in our personal relationships with

other people. It is only when Christ lives in our hearts that bitterness will die and this love will spring to life. It is often said that this world would be perfect if only people would live according to the principles of the Sermon on the Mount; but the plain fact is that no one can even begin to live according to these principles without the help of Jesus Christ. We need Christ to enable us to obey Christ's command.

(6) Last – and it may be most important of all – we must note that this commandment does not only involve allowing people to do as they like to us; it also involves us doing something for them. *We are bidden to pray for them.* No one can pray for others and still hate them. When we take ourselves and those whom we are tempted to hate to God, something happens. We cannot go on hating others in the presence of God. The surest way of killing bitterness is to pray for those whom we are tempted to hate.

2. The reason for it

WE have seen what Jesus meant when he commanded us to have this Christian love; and now we must go on to see why he demanded that we should have it. Why, then, does Jesus demand that people should have this love, this unconquerable benevolence, this invincible goodwill? The reason is very simple and tremendous – it is that such a love makes men and women like God.

Jesus pointed to the action of God in the world, and that is the action of unconquerable benevolence. God makes his sun to rise on the good and the evil; he sends his rain on the just and the unjust. Rabbi Joshua ben Nehemiah used to say: 'Have you ever noticed that the rain fell on the field of A, who was righteous, and not on the field of B, who was wicked? Or that the sun rose and shone on Israel, who was righteous, and not upon the Gentiles, who were wicked? God causes the sun to shine both on Israel and on the nations, for the Lord is good to all.' Even the Jewish Rabbi was moved and impressed with the sheer benevolence of God to saint and sinner alike.

There is a Rabbinic tale which tells of the destruction of the Egyptians in the Red Sea. When the Egyptians were drowned, so the tale runs, the angels began a hymn of praise, but God said sorrowfully: 'The work of my hands are sunk in the sea, and you would sing before me!' The love of God is such that he can never take pleasure in the destruction of any of the creatures whom his hands have made. The psalmist had it: 'The eyes of *all* look to you, and you give them their food in due season. You open your hand, satisfying the desire of *every living thing*' (Psalm 145:15–16). In God there is this universal benevolence even towards those who have broken his law and broken his heart.

Jesus says that we must have this love in order that we may become children of our Father who is in heaven. The word used is literally translated 'sons'. As was noted in the discussion of the beatitudes, Hebrew is not rich in adjectives; and for that reason Hebrew often uses *son of* ... with an abstract noun, where we would use an adjective. For instance, *a son of peace* is *a peaceful man*; *a son of consolation* is *a consoling man*. So, *a son of God* is *a Godlike man*. The reason why we must have this unconquerable benevolence and goodwill is that God has it; and, if we have it, we become nothing less than *children of God, Godlike men and women*.

Here we have the key to one of the most difficult sentences in the New Testament, the sentence with which this passage finishes. Jesus said: 'You, therefore, must be perfect as your heavenly Father is perfect.' On the face of it, that sounds like a commandment which cannot possibly have anything to do with us. There is not one of us who would even faintly connect ourselves with perfection.

The Greek word for *perfect* is *teleios*. This word is often used in Greek in a very special way. It has nothing to do with what we might call abstract, philosophical, metaphysical perfection. A victim which is fit for a sacrifice to God, that is a victim which is without blemish, is *teleios*. A man who has reached his full-grown stature is *teleios* as distinct from a half-grown youth. A student who has reached a mature knowledge of a subject is *teleios* as opposed to a learner who is just beginning, and who as yet has no grasp of things.

To put it in another way, the Greek idea of perfection is *functional*. A thing is perfect if it fully realizes the purpose for which it was planned, designed and made. In point of fact, that meaning is involved in the derivation of the word. *Teleios* is the adjective formed from the noun *telos*. *Telos* means an *end*, a *purpose*, an *aim*, a *goal*. A thing is *teleios* if it achieves the purpose for which it is planned; human beings are perfect if they achieve the purpose for which they were created and sent into the world.

Let us take a very simple analogy. Suppose in my house there is a loose screw, and I want to tighten and adjust this screw. I go out and I buy a screwdriver. I find that the screwdriver exactly fits the grip of my hand; it is neither too large nor too small, too rough nor too smooth. I lay the screwdriver on the slot of the screw, and I find that it exactly fits. I then turn the screw and the screw is fixed. In the Greek sense, and especially in the New Testament sense, that screwdriver is *teleios*, because it exactly fulfilled the purpose for which I desired and bought it.

So, people will be *teleios* if they fulfil the purpose for which they were created. For what purpose were human beings created? The Bible leaves us in no doubt as to that. In the old creation story in the Revised Standard Version translation, we find God saying: 'Let us make man in our image after our likeness' (Genesis 1:26). *Human beings were created to be like God.* The characteristic of God is this universal benevolence, this unconquerable goodwill, this constant seeking of the highest good of every individual. The great characteristic of God is love to saint and to sinner alike. No matter what we do to him, God seeks nothing but our highest good.

Edward Denny's hymn has it of Jesus:

> *Thy foes might hate, despise, revile,*
> *Thy friends unfaithful prove;*
> *Unwearied in forgiveness still,*
> *Thy heart could only love.*

It is when we reproduce in our lives the unwearied, forgiving, sacrificial benevolence of God that we become like God, and are therefore *perfect* in the New Testament sense of the word. To put it at its simplest, those men and women who care most for others are the most perfect.

It is the whole teaching of the Bible that we attain our humanity only by becoming Godlike. The one thing which makes us like God is the love which never ceases to care for others, no matter what they do to it. We fulfil our humanity, we enter upon Christian perfection, when we learn to forgive as God forgives, and to love as God loves.

The story of the loving father

Luke 15:11–32

Jesus said, 'There was a man who had two sons. The younger of them said to his father, "Father, give me the part of the estate which falls to me." So his father divided his living between them. Not many days after, the son realized it all and went away to a far country, and there in wanton recklessness scattered his substance. When he had spent everything a mighty famine arose throughout that country and he began to be in want. He went and attached himself to a citizen of that country, and he sent him into his fields to feed pigs; and he had a great desire to fill himself with the husks the pigs were eating; and no one gave anything to him. When he had come to himself, he said, "How many of my father's hired servants have more than enough bread, and I – I am perishing here with hunger. I will get up and I will go to my father, and I will say to him, 'Father, I have sinned against heaven and before you. I am no longer fit to be called your son. Make me as one of your hired servants.'" So he got up and went to his father. While he was still a long way away his father saw him, and was moved to the depths of his being and ran and flung his arms round his neck and kissed him tenderly. The son said to him, "Father, I have sinned against heaven and before you. I am no longer fit to be called your son." But the father said to his servants, "Quick! Bring out the best robe and put it on

him; put a ring on his finger; put shoes on his feet; and bring
the fatted calf and kill it and let us eat and rejoice, for this
my son was dead and has come back to life again; he was lost
and has been found." And they began to rejoice.

'Now the elder son was in the field. When he came near the
house he heard the sound of music and dancing. He called one
of the slaves and asked what these things could mean. He said
to him, "Your brother has come, and your father has killed
the fatted calf because he has got him back safe and sound."
He was enraged and refused to come in. His father went out
and urged him to come in. He answered his father, "Look you,
I have served you so many years and I never transgressed
your order, and to me you never gave a kid that I might have
a good time with my friends. But when this son of yours – this
fellow who consumed your living with harlots – came, you
killed the fatted calf for him." "Child," he said to him, "you
are always with me. Everything that is mine is yours. But we
had to rejoice and be glad, for your brother was dead and
has come back to life again; he was lost and has been found."'

NOT without reason this has been called the greatest short
story in the world. Under Jewish law a father was not free
to leave his property as he liked. The elder son must get
two-thirds and the younger one-third (Deuteronomy 21:17).
It was by no means unusual for a father to distribute his
estate before he died, if he wished to retire from the actual
management of affairs. But there is a certain heartless
callousness in the request of the younger son. He said in
effect, 'Give me now the part of the estate I will get anyway
when you are dead, and let me get out of this.' The father
did not argue. He knew that if the son was ever to learn he

must learn the hard way; and he granted his request. Without delay the son realized his share of the property and left home.

He soon ran through the money; and he finished up feeding pigs, a task that was forbidden to a Jew because the law said, 'Cursed is he who feeds swine.' Then Jesus paid sinning humanity the greatest compliment it has ever been paid. '*When he came to himself*', he said. Jesus believed that being away from God prevented people from being truly themselves. That was only possible once they were on their way home. Beyond a doubt Jesus did not believe in total depravity. He never believed that you could glorify God by denigrating human beings; he believed that we are never essentially ourselves until we come home to God.

So the son decided to come home and plead to be taken back not as a son but in the lowest rank of slaves, the hired servants, the men who were only day labourers. The ordinary slave was in some sense a member of the family, but the hired servant could be dismissed at a day's notice. He was not one of the family at all. He came home; and, according to the best Greek text, his father never gave him the chance to ask to be a servant. He broke in before that. The robe stands for honour; the ring for authority, for if a man gave to another his signet ring it was the same as giving him the power of attorney; the shoes for a son as opposed to a slave, for children of the family wore shoes and slaves did not. (The slave's dream in the words of the spiritual is of the time when 'all God's chillun got shoes', for shoes were the sign of freedom.) And a feast was made that all might rejoice at the wanderer's return.

Let us stop there and see the truth so far in this parable.

(1) It should never have been called the parable of the prodigal son, for the son is not the hero. It should be called the parable of the loving father, for it tells us rather about a father's love than a son's sin.

(2) It tells us much about the forgiveness of God. The father must have been waiting and watching for the son to come home, for he saw him a long way off. When he came, he forgave him with no recriminations. There is a way of forgiving, when forgiveness is conferred as a favour. It is even worse, when someone is forgiven, but always by hint and by word and by threat the sin is held over them.

Once Abraham Lincoln was asked how he was going to treat the rebellious southerners when they had finally been defeated and had returned to the Union of the United States. The questioner expected that Lincoln would take a dire vengeance, but he answered, 'I will treat them as if they had never been away.'

It is the wonder of the love of God that he treats us like that.

That is not the end of the story. There enters the elder brother who was actually sorry that his brother had come home. He stands for the self-righteous Pharisees who would rather see a sinner destroyed than saved. Certain things stand out about him.

(1) His attitude shows that his years of obedience to his father had been years of grim duty and not of loving service.

(2) His attitude is one of utter lack of sympathy. He refers to the prodigal, not as *my brother* but as *your son*. He was the kind of self-righteous character who would cheerfully have kicked a man farther into the gutter when he was already down.

(3) He had a peculiarly nasty mind. There is no mention of harlots until he mentions them. He, no doubt, suspected his brother of the sins he himself would have liked to commit.

Once again we have the amazing truth that it is easier to confess to God than it is to another person; that God is more merciful in his judgments than many orthodox people; that God's love is far broader than human love; and that God can forgive when we refuse to forgive. In face of a love like that we cannot be other than lost in wonder, love and praise.

Love's extravagance

John 12:1–8

> Now six days before the Passover Jesus went to Bethany, where
> Lazarus was whom he raised from the dead. So they made
> him a meal there, and Martha was serving while Lazarus was
> one of those who reclined at table with him. Now Mary took
> a pound of very precious genuine spikenard ointment, and
> anointed Jesus' feet, and wiped his feet with her hair; and the
> house was filled with the perfume of the ointment. But Judas
> Iscariot, one of his disciples, the one who was going to betray
> him, said: 'Why was this ointment not sold for ten pounds, and
> the proceeds given to the poor?' He said this, not that he cared
> for the poor, but because he was a thief and had charge of the
> money box, and pilfered from what was put into it. So Jesus
> said: 'Let her observe it now against the day of my burial. The
> poor you have always with you, but me you have not always.'

IT was coming very near the end for Jesus. To come to
Jerusalem for the Passover was an act of the highest courage,
for the authorities had made him in effect an outlaw (John
11:57). So great were the crowds who came to the Passover
that they could not all possibly obtain lodging within the
city itself, and Bethany was one of the places outside the
city boundaries which the law laid down as a place for the
overflow of the pilgrims to stay.

When Jesus came to Bethany, they made him a meal. It must have been in the house of Martha and Mary and their brother Lazarus, for where else would Martha be serving but in her own house? It was then that Mary's heart ran over in love. She had a pound of very precious spikenard (an aromatic herb) ointment. Both John and Mark describe it by the adjective *pistikos* (Mark 14:3). Oddly enough, no one really knows what that word means. There are four possibilities. It may come from the adjective *pistos* which means *faithful* or *reliable*, and so may mean *genuine*. It may come from the verb *pinein* which means *to drink*, and so may mean *liquid*. It may be a kind of trade name, and may have to be translated simply *pistic nard*. It may come from a word meaning the *pistachio nut*, and be a special kind of essence extracted from it. In any event, it was a specially valuable kind of perfume. With this perfume, Mary anointed Jesus' feet. Judas ungraciously questioned her action as sheer waste. Jesus silenced him by saying that money could be given to the poor at any time, but a kindness done to him must be done now, for soon the chance would be gone forever.

There is a whole series of little character sketches here.

(1) There is the character of Martha. She was serving at table. She loved Jesus; she was a practical woman; and the only way in which she could show her love was by the work of her hands. Martha always gave what she could. Many great men and women have been what they were only because of someone's loving care for their creature comforts in the home. It is just as possible to serve Jesus in the kitchen as on the public platform or in a career lived in the public gaze.

(2) There is the character of Mary. Mary was the one who above all loved Jesus; and here in her action we see three things about love.

(a) We see love's extravagance. Mary took the most precious thing she possessed and spent it all on Jesus. Love is not love if it nicely calculates the cost. It gives its all, and its only regret is that it has not still more to give. O. Henry, the master of the short story, has a moving story called *The Gift of the Magi*. A young American couple, Della and Jim, were very poor but very much in love. Each had one unique possession. Della's hair was her glory. When she let it down, it almost served as a robe. Jim had a gold watch which had come to him from his father and was his pride. It was the day before Christmas, and Della had exactly one dollar eighty-seven cents to buy Jim a present. She went out and sold her hair for twenty dollars, and with the proceeds bought a platinum fob for Jim's precious watch. When Jim came home at night and saw Della's shorn head, he stopped as if stupefied. It was not that he did not like it or that he no longer loved her; for she was lovelier than ever. Slowly he handed her his gift; it was a set of expensive tortoise-shell combs with jewelled edges for her lovely hair – and he had sold his gold watch to buy them. Each had given the other all there was to give. Real love cannot think of any other way to give.

(b) We see love's humility. It was a sign of honour to anoint a person's head. 'You anoint my head with oil,' says the psalmist (Psalm 23:5). But Mary would not look so high as the head of Jesus; she anointed his feet. The last thing Mary thought of was to confer an honour upon Jesus; she never dreamed she was good enough for that.

(c) We see love's unselfconsciousness. Mary wiped Jesus' feet with the hair of her head. In Palestine, no respectable woman would ever appear in public with her hair unbound. On the day a girl was married, her hair was bound up, and never again would she be seen in public with her long tresses flowing loose. That was the sign of an immoral woman. But Mary never even thought of that. When two people really love each other, they live in a world of their own. They will wander slowly down a crowded street hand in hand, heedless of what other people think. Many are self-conscious about showing their Christianity, concerned always about what others are thinking about them. Mary loved Jesus so much that it was nothing to her what others thought.

But there is something else about love here. John has the sentence: 'The house was filled with the fragrance of the ointment.' We have seen that so many of John's statements have two meanings, one which lies on the surface and one which is underneath. Many fathers of the Church and many scholars have seen a double meaning here. They have taken it to mean that the whole Church was filled with the sweet memory of Mary's action. A lovely deed becomes the possession of the whole world and adds to the beauty of life in general, something which time cannot ever take away.

The farewell command

John 13:33–5

'Little children, I am still going to be with you for a little while. You will search for me; and, as I said to the Jews, so now I say to you too: "You cannot go where I am going." I give you a new commandment, that you love one another; that you too love one another, as I have loved you; it is by this that all will know that you are my disciples – if you have love among each other.'

JESUS was laying down his farewell commandment to his disciples. The time was short; if they were ever to hear his voice, they must hear it now. He was going on a journey on which none might accompany him; he was taking a road that he had to walk alone; and before he went, he gave them the commandment that they must love one another as he had loved them. What does this mean for us, and for our relationships with one another? How did Jesus love his disciples?

(1) He loved his disciples *selflessly*. Even in the noblest human love, there remains some element of self. We so often think – maybe unconsciously – of what we are to get. We think of the happiness we will receive, or of the loneliness we will suffer if love fails or is denied. So often we are thinking, what will this love do for me? So often at the back of things it is *our* happiness that we are seeking. But Jesus never thought of himself. His one desire was to give himself and all he had for those he loved.

(2) Jesus loved his disciples *sacrificially*. There was no limit to what his love would give or to where it would go. No demand that could be made upon it was too much. If love meant the cross, Jesus was prepared to go there. Sometimes we make the mistake of thinking that love is meant to give us happiness. So in the end it does, but love may well bring pain and demand a cross.

(3) Jesus loved his disciples *understandingly*. He knew his disciples through and through. We never really know people until we have lived with them. When we are meeting them only occasionally, we see them at their best. It is when we live with them that we find out their moods and their irritabilities and their weaknesses. Jesus had lived with his disciples day in and day out for many months and knew all that was to be known about them – and he still loved them. Sometimes we say that love is blind. That is not so, for the love that is blind can end in nothing but bleak and utter disillusionment. Real love is open-eyed. It loves, not what it imagines people to be, but what they are. The heart of Jesus is big enough to love us as we are.

(4) Jesus loved his disciples *forgivingly*. Their leader was to deny him. They were all to forsake him in his hour of need. They never really understood him. They were blind and insensitive, slow to learn, and lacking in understanding. In the end, they were miserable cowards. But Jesus held nothing against them; there was no failure which he could not forgive. The love which has not learned to forgive cannot do anything else but shrivel and die. We are poor creatures, and there is a kind of fate in things which makes us hurt most of all those who love us best. For that very reason, all enduring love must be built on forgiveness, for without forgiveness it is bound to die.

The hymn of love

1 Corinthians 13

I may speak with the tongues of men and of angels, but if I have not love, I am become no better than echoing brass or a clanging cymbal. I may have the gift of prophecy, I may understand all sacred secrets and all knowledge, I may have faith enough to remove mountains, but if I have not love I am nothing. I may dole out all that I have, I may surrender my body that I may be burned, but if I have not love it is no good to me.

Love is patient; love is kind; love knows no envy; love is no braggart; it is not inflated with its own importance; it does not behave gracelessly; it does not insist on its rights; it never flies into a temper; it does not store up the memory of any wrong it has received; it finds no pleasure in evildoing; it rejoices with the truth; it can endure anything; it is completely trusting; it never ceases to hope; it bears everything with triumphant fortitude.

Love never fails. Whatever prophecies there are, they will vanish away. Whatever tongues there are, they will cease. Whatever knowledge we have, it will pass away. It is only part of the truth that we know now and only part of the truth that we can forthtell to others. But when that which is complete shall come, that which is incomplete will vanish away. When I was a child, I used to speak like a child; I

used to think like a child; I used to reason like a child. When
I became a man, I put an end to childish things. Now we
see only reflections in a mirror which leave us with nothing
but riddles to solve, but then we shall see face to face. Now
I know in part; but then I will know even as I am known.
Now faith, hope, love remain – these three; but the greatest
of these is love.

FOR many, this is the most wonderful chapter in the whole
New Testament; and we will do well to take our time in
studying words the full meaning of which could not be
sufficiently revealed in a whole lifetime.

Paul begins by declaring that we may possess any spiritual
gift, but if it is unaccompanied by love it is useless.

(1) Some may have the gift of *tongues*. A characteristic of
Gentile worship, especially the worship of the Greek god of
wine, Dionysus, and of the goddess Cybele, was the clanging
of cymbals and the blaring of trumpets. Even the coveted gift
of tongues was no better than the uproar of Gentile worship
if love was absent.

(2) Some may have the gift of *prophecy*. Prophecy
corresponds most closely to preaching. There are two
kinds of preachers. There are preachers whose one aim
is to save souls and who woo people with the accents of
love. Of no one was that more true than of Paul himself.
F. W. H. Myers, in his poem 'Saint Paul', draws the picture of
him looking at the Christless world:

> *Then with a thrill the intolerable craving*
> *Shivers throughout me like a trumpet call –*
> *O to save these – to perish for their saving –*
> *Die for their lives, be offered for them all.*

On the other hand, there are preachers who dangle their hearers over the flames of hell and give the impression that they would rejoice in their damnation as much as in their salvation. The preaching which is all threat and no love may terrify, but it will not save.

(3) Some may have the gift of *intellectual knowledge*. The permanent danger of intellectual distinction is intellectual snobbery. People who have great knowledge run the grave danger of developing the spirit of contempt. Only a knowledge whose cold detachment has been set alight by the fire of love can really save men and women.

(4) Some may have a passionate *faith*. There are times when faith can be cruel. There was a man who visited his doctor and was informed that his heart was tired and he must rest. He telephoned his employer, a notable Christian figure, with the news, only to receive the answer: 'I have an inward strength which enables me to carry on.' These were the words of faith, but a faith which knew no love and therefore gave pain and hurt.

(5) Some may practise *charity*; they may distribute their goods to the poor. There is nothing more humiliating than this so-called charity without love. To give as a grim duty, to give with a certain contempt, to take the moral high ground and throw scraps of charity as to a dog, to give and to accompany the giving with a smug moral lecture or a crushing rebuke, is not charity at all – it is pride; and pride is always cruel, for it knows no love.

(6) Some may give their bodies to be burned. Possibly, Paul's thoughts are going back to Shadrach, Meshach and Abednego and the burning fiery furnace (Daniel 3). It is perhaps more likely that he is thinking of a famous monument

in Athens called 'the Indian's Tomb'. There, an Indian had burned himself in public on a funeral pyre and had arranged to have engraved on the monument the boastful inscription: 'Zarmano-chegas, an Indian from Bargosa, according to the traditional customs of the Indians, made himself immortal and lies here.' Just possibly, Paul may have been thinking of the kind of Christian who actually courted persecution. If the motive which makes people give their lives for Christ is pride and exhibitionism, then even martyrdom becomes valueless. It is not cynical to remember that many actions which look sacrificial have been the product of pride and not of devotion.

Hardly any passage in Scripture demands such self-examination as this from those who consider themselves to be good.

The nature of Christian love

1 Corinthians 13:4–7

In verses 4–7, Paul lists fifteen characteristics of Christian love.

Love is patient. The Greek word (*makrothumein*) used in the New Testament always describes patience with *people* and not patience with circumstances. The fourth-century Church father John Chrysostom said that it is the word used of those who are wronged and who have it easily in their power to avenge themselves and yet who will not do it. It describes people who are slow to anger, and it is used of God himself in his relationship with men and women. In our dealings with others, however difficult and however unkind and hurting they are, we must exercise the same patience as God exercises with us. Such patience is not the sign of weakness but the sign of strength; it is not defeatism but rather the only way to victory. The American Baptist Harry Emerson Fosdick points out that no one treated the President, Abraham Lincoln, with more contempt than did his secretary for war, Edwin Stanton. He called him 'a low cunning clown', he nicknamed him 'the original gorilla' and said that the traveller and explorer Paul Du Chaillu was a fool to wander about Africa trying to capture a gorilla when he could have found one so easily at Springfield, Illinois. Lincoln said nothing. He made Stanton his war minister because he was the best man for the job, and he treated him with every courtesy. The years wore on. The night came when the assassin's bullet murdered Lincoln in the theatre. In the little room to which the President's body was taken stood that same Stanton, and, looking down on Lincoln's silent face, he said through his tears: 'There lies the greatest ruler of men the world has ever seen.' The patience of love had conquered in the end.

Love is kind. The third-century biblical scholar Origen had it that this means that love is 'sweet to all'. Writing about a century later, Jerome spoke of what he called 'the benignity' of love. So much Christianity is good but unkind. There was no one more religious than Philip II of Spain, and yet he founded the Spanish Inquisition and thought he was serving God by massacring those who thought differently from him. The famous Cardinal Pole declared that murder and adultery could not compare in wickedness with heresy. Quite apart from that persecuting spirit, there is in so many good people an attitude of criticism. So many good church people would have sided with the rulers and not with Jesus if they had had to deal with the woman taken in adultery (see John 8:1–11).

Love knows no envy. It has been said that there are really only two classes of people in this world – 'those who are millionaires and those who would like to be'. There are two kinds of envy. The one covets the possessions of other people; and such envy is very difficult to avoid, because it is a very human failing. The other is worse – it grudges the very fact that others should have what it has not; it does not so much want things for itself as wish that others had not got them. Meanness of soul can sink no further than that.

Love is no braggart. Love is not boastful. There is a self-effacing quality in love. True love will always be far more impressed with its own unworthiness than its own merit. In the writer J. M. Barrie's story, Sentimental Tommy used to come home to his mother after some success at school and say: 'Mother, am I no' a wonder?' Some people confer their love with the idea that they are conferring a favour. But people who really love cannot get over the wonder that they are loved. Love is kept humble by the consciousness that it can never offer its loved one a gift which is good enough.

Love is not inflated with its own importance. Napoleon always advocated the sanctity of the home and the obligation of public worship – for others. Of himself, he said: 'I am not a man like other men. The laws of morality do not apply to me.' Really great people never think of their own importance. William Carey, who began life mending shoes as a cobbler, was one of the greatest missionaries and certainly one of the greatest linguists the world has ever seen. He translated some parts of the Bible into no fewer than thirty-four Indian languages. When he came to India, he was regarded with dislike and contempt. At a dinner party, a snob, with the idea of humiliating him, said in a tone that everyone could hear: 'I suppose, Mr Carey, you once worked as a shoemaker.' 'No, your lordship,' answered Carey, 'not a shoemaker, only a cobbler.' He did not even claim to make shoes – only to mend them. No one likes the 'important' person. It can be a sorry sight to see, as Shakespeare had it, 'man dressed in a little brief authority'.

Love does not behave gracelessly. It is a significant fact that in Greek the words for *grace* and for *charm* are the same. There is a kind of Christianity which takes a delight in being blunt and almost brutal. There is strength in it, but there is no grace or charm. Bishop J. B. Lightfoot of Durham said of Arthur F. Sim, one of his students: 'Let him go where he will, his face will be a sermon in itself.' There is a graciousness in Christian love which never forgets that courtesy and tact and politeness are lovely things.

Love does not insist upon its rights. In the last analysis, there are in this world only two kinds of people – those who always insist upon their privileges and those who always remember their responsibilities; those who are always thinking of what life owes them and those who never forget what they owe to life. It would be the key to almost all the problems which surround us today if people would think less of their rights and more of their duties. Whenever we start thinking about 'our place', we are drifting away from Christian love.

Love never flies into a temper. The real meaning of this is that Christian love never becomes exasperated with people. Exasperation is always a sign of defeat. When we lose our tempers, we lose everything. In his famous poem, 'If', Rudyard Kipling said that it was the test of a man if he could keep his head when everyone else was losing his and blaming it on him, and if when he was hated he did not give way to hating. Those who can control their tempers can overcome anything.

Love does not store up the memory of any wrong it has received. The word translated as *store up* (*logizesthai*) is an accountant's word. It is the word used for entering up an item in a ledger so that it will not be forgotten. That is precisely what so many people do. One of the great arts in life is to learn what to forget. Similarly, many people nurse their anger to keep it simmering; they brood over their wrongs until it is impossible to forget them. Christian love has learned the great lesson of forgetting.

Love finds no pleasure in evildoing. It might be better to translate this sentence as *love finds no pleasure in anything that is wrong*. It is not so much delight in doing the wrong thing that is meant, as the malicious pleasure which comes to most of us when we hear something derogatory about someone else. It is one of the strange features of human nature that very often we prefer to hear of the misfortune of others rather than of their good fortune. It is much easier to weep with those who weep than to rejoice with those who rejoice. Christian love has none of that human malice which finds pleasure in hearing unpleasant things about other people.

Love rejoices with the truth. That is not as easy as it sounds. There are times when we definitely do not want the truth to prevail, and still more times when it is the last thing we wish to hear. Christian love has no wish to conceal the truth; it has nothing to hide and so is glad when the truth wins through.

Love can endure anything. It is just possible that this may mean 'love can cover anything', in the sense that it will never drag into the light of day the faults and mistakes of others. It would far rather set about quietly mending things than publicly displaying and rebuking them. More likely, it means that love can bear any insult, any injury, any disappointment. It describes the kind of love that was in the heart of Jesus himself. As Edward Denny's hymn has it:

> *Thy foes might hate, despise, revile,*
> *Thy friends unfaithful prove;*

Unwearied in forgiveness still,
Thy heart could only love.

Love is completely trusting. This characteristic has a two-fold aspect. (1) *In relation to God*, it means that love takes God at his word, and can take every promise which begins 'Whoever' and say: 'That means me.' (2) *In relation to our fellow men and women*, it means that love always believes the best about other people. It is often true that we make people what we believe them to be. If we show that we do not trust people, we may make them untrustworthy. If we show people that we trust them absolutely, we may make them trustworthy. When Thomas Arnold became headmaster of Rugby School in 1828, he instituted a completely new way of doing things. Before he arrived, school had been a terror and a tyranny. Arnold called the boys together and told them that there was going to be much more liberty and much less flogging. 'You are free,' he said, 'but you are responsible – you are gentlemen. I intend to leave you much to yourselves, and put you upon your honour, because I believe that if you are guarded and watched and spied upon, you will grow up knowing only the fruits of servile fear; and when your liberty is finally given you, as it must be some day, you will not know how to use it.' The boys found it difficult to believe. When they were brought before him, they continued to make the old excuses and to tell the old lies. 'Boys,' he said, 'if you say so, it must be true – I believe your word.' The result was that there came a time in Rugby when boys said: 'It is a shame to tell Arnold a lie – he always believes you.' He believed in them, and he made them what he believed them to be. Love can make honourable even the dishonourable by believing the best.

Love never ceases to hope. Jesus believed that no one is beyond hope. The Methodist Adam Clarke was one of the great theologians, but at school he was very slow to learn. One day, a distinguished visitor paid a visit to the school, and the teacher singled out Adam Clarke and said: 'That is the stupidest boy in the school.' Before he left the school, the visitor came to the boy and said kindly: 'Never mind, my boy, you may be a great scholar some day. Don't be discouraged but try hard, and keep on trying.' The teacher had no hope; but the visitor was hopeful, and – who knows? – it may well have been that word of hope which made Adam Clarke what he one day became.

Love bears everything with triumphant fortitude. The verb used here (*hupomenein*) is one of the great Greek words. It is generally translated as *to bear* or *to endure*; but what it really describes is not the spirit which can passively bear things, but the spirit which, in bearing them, can conquer and change their very nature. The Scottish minister and hymn-writer George Matheson, who lost his sight and who was disappointed in love, wrote in one of his prayers that he might accept God's will 'Not with dumb resignation but with holy joy; not only with the absence of murmur but with a song of praise.' Love can bear things not merely with passive resignation, but with triumphant fortitude, because it knows that 'a father's hand will never cause his child a needless tear'.

One thing remains to be said: when we think of the qualities of this love as Paul portrays them, we can see them made real in the life of Jesus himself.

The supremacy of love

1 Corinthians 13:8–13

In verses 8–13, Paul has three final things to say of this Christian love.

(1) He stresses its *absolute permanency*. When all the things in which people take pride and delight have passed away, love will still stand. In one of the most wonderfully lyrical verses of Scripture, the Song of Solomon (8:7) sings: 'Many waters cannot quench love, neither can floods drown it.' The one unconquerable thing is love. That is one of the great reasons for believing in immortality. When love is entered into, there comes into life a relationship against which the assaults of time are helpless and which transcends death.

(2) He stresses its *absolute completeness*. As things are, what we see are reflections in a mirror. That image presented in this statement would be even more vivid for the Corinthians than it is for us. Corinth was famous for its manufacture of mirrors. But the modern mirror as we know it, with its perfect reflection, did not emerge until the thirteenth century. The Corinthian mirror was made of highly polished metal and, even at its best, gave but an imperfect reflection. It has been suggested that what this phrase means is that we see as through a window made with horn. That was the material used for making windows

in those days, and all that could be seen through them was a dim and shadowy outline. In fact, the Rabbis had a saying that it was through such a window that Moses saw God.

In this life, Paul feels that we see only the reflections of God and are left with much that is mystery and riddle. We see that reflection in God's world, for the work of anyone's hands tells us something about the one who has done that work. We see it in the gospel, and we see it in Jesus Christ. Even if in Christ we have the perfect revelation, our searching and inquiring minds can grasp it only in part, for the finite can never grasp the infinite. Our knowledge is still like the knowledge of a child. But the way of love will lead us in the end to a day when the veil is drawn aside and we see face to face and know even as we are known. We cannot ever reach that day without love, because God is love, and only those who love can see him.

(3) He stresses its *absolute supremacy*. Great as faith and hope are, love is still greater. Faith without love is cold, and hope without love is grim. Love is the fire which gives the spark to faith, and it is the light which turns hope into certainty.

The love from which nothing can separate us

Romans 8:31–9

What then shall we say to these things? If God is for us, who is against us? The very God who did not spare his own Son but who delivered him up for us all, how shall he not with him also freely give us all things? Who shall impeach the elect of God? It is God who acquits. Who is he who condemns? It is Jesus Christ who died, nay, rather, who was raised from the dead, and who is at the right hand of God, who also intercedes for us. Who will separate us from the love of Christ? Shall trial, or distress, or persecution, or famine, or nakedness, or peril, or sword? As it stands written, 'For Thy sake we are killed all the day long; we are reckoned as sheep for the slaughter.' But in all these things we are more than conquerors through him who loved us. For I am convinced that neither death, nor life, nor angels, nor principalities, nor the present age, nor the age to come, nor powers, nor height, nor depth, nor any other creation will be able to separate us from the love of God which is in Christ Jesus our Lord.

THIS is one of the most lyrical passages Paul ever wrote. In verse 32, there is a wonderful allusion which would stand out to any Jew who knew the Old Testament well. Paul says in effect: 'God for us did not spare his own Son; surely that is the final guarantee that he loves us enough to supply all our needs.' The words Paul uses of God are the very words God used of Abraham when Abraham proved his utter loyalty by being willing to sacrifice his son Isaac at God's command. God said to Abraham: 'You have not withheld your son, your only son, from me' (Genesis 22:12). Paul seems to say: 'Think of the greatest human example in the world of an individual's loyalty to God; God's loyalty to you is like that.' Just as Abraham was so loyal to God that he was prepared to sacrifice his dearest possession, God is so loyal to men and women that he is prepared to sacrifice his only Son for them. Surely we can trust a loyalty like that for anything.

It is difficult to know just how to take verses 33–5. There are two ways of taking them; and both give excellent sense and precious truth.

(1) We can take them as two statements, followed by two questions which give the inferences to be made from these statements. (a) It is God who acquits us – that is the statement. If that is so, who can possibly condemn us? If we are acquitted by God, then we are saved from every other condemnation. (b) Our belief is in a Christ who died and rose again and who is alive for evermore – that is the statement. If that is so, is there anything in this or any other world that can separate us from our risen Lord?

If we take it that way, two great truths are laid down. (a) God has acquitted us; therefore no one can condemn us. (b) Christ is risen; therefore nothing can ever separate us from him.

(2) But there is another way to take it. God has acquitted us. Who then can condemn us? The answer is that the judge of all is Jesus Christ. He is the one who has the right

to condemn – but, far from condemning, he is at God's right hand interceding for us, and therefore we are safe.

It may be that, in verse 34, Paul is doing a very wonderful thing. He is saying four things about Jesus. (a) He died. (b) He rose again. (c) He is at the right hand of God. (d) He makes intercession for us there. Now, the earliest creed of the Church, which is still the essence of all Christian creeds, ran like this: 'He was crucified dead and buried; the third day he rose again from the dead; and sitteth at the right hand of God; *from thence he shall come to judge the quick* [living] *and the dead.*' Three items in Paul's statement and in the early creed are the same, that Jesus died, rose again, and is at the right hand of God. *But the fourth is different.* In the creed, the fourth is that Jesus will come *to be the judge of the quick and the dead.* In Paul, the fourth is that Jesus is at God's right hand *to plead our case.* It is as if Paul said: 'You think of Jesus as the judge who is there to condemn; and well he might, for he has won the right. But you are wrong; he is not there to be our prosecuting counsel but to be the advocate to plead our cause.'

I think that the second way of taking this is right. With one tremendous leap of thought, Paul has seen Christ not as the judge but as the lover of human souls.

Paul goes on with a poet's fervour and a lover's rapture to sing of how nothing can separate us from the love of God in our risen Lord.

(1) No affliction, no hardship, no peril can separate us (verse 35). The disasters of the world do not separate us from Christ; they bring us closer.

(2) In verses 38–9, Paul makes a list of terrible things.

Neither *life nor death* can separate us from Christ. In life we live with Christ; in death we die with him; and because we die with him, we also rise with him. Death, far from being a separation, is only a step into his nearer presence; not the end but 'the gate on the skyline' leading to the presence of Jesus Christ.

The angelic powers cannot separate us from him. At this particular time, the Jews had a highly developed belief in angels. Everything had its angel. There was an angel of the winds, of the clouds, of the snow and hail and hoar frost, of the thunder and the lightning, of cold and heat and of the seasons. The Rabbis said that there was nothing in the world, not even a blade of grass, that did not have its angel. According to the Rabbis, there were three ranks of angels. The first included thrones, cherubim and seraphim. The second included powers, lordships and mights. The third included angels, archangels and principalities. More than once, Paul speaks of these angels (Ephesians 1:21, 3:10, 6:12; Colossians 2:10, 2:15; 1 Corinthians 15:24). Now, the Rabbis – and Paul had once been a Rabbi – believed that they were grudgingly hostile to men and women. They believed that they had been angry when God created human life. It was as if they did not want to share God with anyone and had grudged human beings their share in him. The Rabbis had a legend that, when God appeared on Sinai to give Moses the law, he was attended by his hosts of angels; and the angels grudged Israel the law, and assaulted Moses on his way up the mountain and would have stopped him had not God intervened. So Paul, thinking in terms of his own day, says: 'Not even the grudging, jealous angels can separate us from the love of God, much as they would like to do so.'

No age in time can separate us from Christ. Paul speaks of *things present and things to come*. We know that the Jews divided all time into *this present age* and *the age to come*. Paul is saying: 'In this present world, nothing can separate us from God in Christ; the day will come when this world will be shattered and the new age will dawn. It does not matter; even then, when this world has passed and the new world come, the bond is still the same.'

No malign influences (powers) will separate us from Christ. Paul speaks about *height and depth*. These are astrological terms. The ancient world was haunted by the tyranny of the stars. It was generally believed that everyone was born under a certain star and thereby an individual's destiny was settled. There are some who still believe that; but the ancient world was really haunted by this supposed domination of people's lives by the influence of the stars. *Height* (*hupsōma*) was the time when a star was at its zenith and its influence was greatest; *depth* (*hathos*) was the time when a star was at its lowest, waiting to rise and to put its influence on someone. Paul says to these haunted people of his age: 'The stars cannot hurt you. In their rising and their setting, they are powerless to separate you from God's love.'

No other world can separate us from God. The word that Paul uses for *other* (*heteros*) has really the meaning of *different*. He is saying: 'Suppose that by some wild flight of imagination there emerged another and a different world, you would still be safe; you would still be enfolded in the love of God.'

Here is a vision to take away all loneliness and all fear. Paul is saying: 'You can think of every terrifying thing that this or any other world can produce. Not one of them is able to separate the Christian from the love of God which is in Jesus Christ, Lord of every terror and Master of every world.' Of what then shall we be afraid?

The debts which must be paid and the debt which can never be paid

Romans 13:7–10

Give to all men what is due to them. Give tribute to those to whom tribute is due; pay taxes to those to whom taxes are due. Give fear to those to whom fear is due. Give honour to those to whom honour is due.

Owe no man anything, except to love each other; for he who loves the other man has fulfilled the law. The commandments, You must not commit adultery, You must not kill, You must not steal, You must not covet, and any other commandment there may be, are all summed up in this saying – You must love your neighbour as yourself. Love does no harm to its neighbour. Love is, therefore, the complete fulfilment of the law.

VERSE 7 mentions what might be called public debts. There is what Paul calls *tribute*, and what he calls *taxes*. By *tribute*, he means the tribute that must be paid by those who are members of a nation that is under the rule of another. The standard contributions that the Roman government levied on such nations were three. There was a *ground tax* by which people had to pay, either in cash or in kind, one-tenth of all the grain, and one-fifth of the wine and fruit produced by their land. There was *income tax*, which was one per cent of a man's income. There was a *poll tax*, which had to be paid by everyone between the ages of 14 and 65. By *taxes*, Paul means the local taxes that had to be paid. There were customs duties, import and export taxes, taxes for the use of main roads, for crossing bridges, for entry into markets and harbours, for the right to possess an animal or to drive a cart or wagon. Paul insists that Christians must pay their tribute and their taxes to state and to local authority, however galling it might be.

Then he turns to *private* debts. He says: 'Owe no one anything.' It seems almost unnecessary to say such a thing; but there were some who even twisted the petition of the Lord's Prayer, 'Forgive us our debts, as we forgive our debtors,' into a reason for claiming to be absolved from all money obligations. Paul had to remind his people that Christianity is not an excuse for refusing our obligations to other people; it is a reason for fulfilling them to the utmost.

He goes on to speak of the one debt that must be paid every day, and yet, at the same time, must continue to be owed every day – the debt to love one another. Origen, the great third-century biblical scholar, said: 'The debt of love remains with us permanently and never leaves us; this is a debt which we both discharge every day and forever owe.' It is Paul's claim that if people honestly seek to discharge this debt of love, they will automatically keep all the commandments. They will not commit adultery, for, when two people allow their physical passions to sweep them away, the reason is not that they love each other too much but that they love each other too little. In real love, there is at the same time respect and restraint, which saves from sin. Christians will not kill, for love never seeks to destroy, but always to build up; it is always kind and will always seek to destroy enemies not by killing them, but by seeking to make friends of them. Christians will never steal, for love is always more concerned with giving than with getting. They will not covet, for covetousness (*epithumia*) is the uncontrolled desire for what is forbidden, and love cleanses the heart, until that desire is gone.

St Augustine famously said: 'Love God, and do what you like.' If love is the motivation within the heart, if a person's whole life is dominated by love for God and love for other people, that person needs no other law.

The infinite love of Christ

Ephesians 3:18–21

> I pray that you may have your root and your foundation in love, so that, with all God's consecrated people, you may have the strength fully to grasp the meaning of the breadth and length and depth and height of Christ's love, and to know the love of Christ which is beyond all knowledge, that you may be filled until you reach the fullness of God himself.
>
> To him that is able to do exceeding abundantly, above all that we ask or think, according to the power which works in us, to him be glory in the Church and in Christ Jesus to all generations forever and ever. Amen.

PAUL prays that Christians may be able to grasp the meaning of the breadth, depth, length and height of the love of Christ. It is as if Paul invited us to look at the universe – to the limitless sky above, to the limitless horizons on every side, to the depth of the earth and of the seas beneath us, and said: 'The love of Christ is as vast as that.'

It is unlikely that Paul had any more definite thought in his mind than the sheer vastness of the love of Christ. But many people have taken this picture and have read meanings, some of them very beautiful, into it. One ancient commentator sees the cross as the symbol of this love. The upper arm of the cross points up; the lower arm points down; and the crossing arms point out to the widest horizons.

The fourth-century biblical scholar Jerome said that the love of Christ reaches up to include the holy angels, that it reaches down to include even the evil spirits in hell, that in its length it covers all who are striving on the upward way, and in its breadth it covers those who are wandering away from Christ.

If we want to work this out, we might say that in the *breadth* of its sweep, the love of Christ includes every individual of every kind in every age in every world; in the *length* to which it would go, the love of Christ accepted even the cross; in its *depth*, it descended to experience even death; in its *height*, he still loves us in heaven, where he lives always to make intercession for us (Hebrews 7:25). No one is outside the love of Christ; no place is beyond its reach.

Then Paul comes back again to the thought which dominates this letter. Where is that love to be experienced? We experience it *with all God's consecrated people*. That is to say, we find it in the fellowship of the Church. The founder of Methodism, John Wesley, had a saying which was true: 'God knows nothing of solitary religion.' 'No man', he said, 'ever went to heaven alone.' The Church may have its faults; church members may be very far from what they ought to be; but in the fellowship of the Church we find the love of God.

Paul ends with a hymn of praise to God, who can do for us more than we can dream of, and who does it for us in the Church and in Christ.

Let us think of Paul's glorious picture of the Church. This world is not what it was meant to be; it is torn apart by opposing forces and by hatred and bitter conflict. Nation is against nation, neighbour is against neighbour, class is against class. Within every individual, the fight rages between the evil and the good. It is God's design that all people and all nations should become one in Christ. To achieve this end, Christ needs the Church to go out and tell the world of his love and of his mercy. And the Church cannot do that until its members, joined together in fellowship, experience the limitless love of Christ.

Love human and divine

1 John 4:7–21

Beloved, let us love one another, because love has its source in God, and everyone who loves has God as the source of his birth and knows God. He who does not love has not come to know God. In this, God's love is displayed within us, that God sent his only Son into the world that through him we might live. In this is love, not that we love God, but that he loved us and sent his Son to be an atoning sacrifice for our sins. Brothers, if God so loved us, we too ought to love each other. No one has ever seen God. If we love each other, God dwells in us and his love is perfected in us. It is by this that we know that we dwell in him and he in us, because he has given us a share of his Spirit. We have seen and we testify that the Father sent the Son as the Saviour of the world. Whoever openly acknowledges that Jesus is the Son of God, God dwells in him and he in God. We have come to know and to put our trust in the love which God has within us. God is love, and he who dwells in love dwells in God and God dwells in him. With us, love finds its peak in this, that we should have confidence in the day of judgment because, even as he is, so also are we in this world. There is no fear in love; but perfect love casts out fear, for fear is connected with punishment, and he who fears has not reached love's perfect state. We love because he first loved us. If anyone says 'I love God' and hates his brother, he is a liar; for he who does not love his brother, whom he has seen, cannot love God whom he has not seen. It is this command that we have from him, that he who loves God loves his brother also.

THIS passage is so closely interwoven that it is best to read as a whole and then bit by bit to draw out its teaching. First of all, let us look at its teaching on love.

(1) Love has its origin in God (verse 7). It is from the God who is love that all love takes its source. As A. E. Brooke puts it, 'Human love is a reflection of something in the divine nature itself.' We are never nearer to God than when we love. Clement of Alexandria said, in a startling phrase, that the real Christian 'practises being God'. Those who dwell in love dwell in God (verse 16). We are made in the image and the likeness of God (Genesis 1:26). God is love; and, therefore, to be like God and be what we were meant to be, we must also love.

(2) Love has a double relationship to God. It is only by knowing God that we learn to love, and it is only by loving that we learn to know God (verses 7–8). Love comes from God, and love leads to God.

(3) It is by love that God is known (verse 12). We cannot see God, because he is spirit; what we can see is his effect. We cannot see the wind, but we can see what it can do. We cannot see electricity, but we can see the effect it produces. The effect of God is love. It is when God comes into an individual that that person is clothed with the love of God and the love of other people. God is known by his effect on that individual. It has been said that 'a saint is someone in whom Christ lives again'; and the best demonstration of God comes not from argument but from a life of love.

(4) God's love is demonstrated in Jesus Christ (verse 9). When we look at Jesus, we see two things about the love of God. (a) It is a love which holds nothing back. In his love for men and women, God was prepared to give his only Son and make a sacrifice beyond which no sacrifice can possibly go. (b) It is a totally undeserved love. It would be no wonder if we loved God, when we remember all the gifts he has given to us, even apart from Jesus Christ; the wonder is that he loves poor and disobedient creatures like us. As F. W. Faber's hymn has it,

> *How thou canst think so well of us,*
> *And be the God thou art,*
> *Is darkness to my intellect,*
> *But sunshine to my heart.*

(5) Human love is a response to divine love (verse 19). We love because God loved us. It is the sight of his love which wakens in us the desire to love him as he first loved us and to love our neighbours as he loves them.

(6) When love comes, fear goes (verses 17–18). Fear is the characteristic emotion of someone who expects to be punished. As long as we regard God as the Judge, the King and the Law-giver, there can be nothing in our hearts but fear, for from such a God we can expect nothing but punishment. But once we know God's true nature, fear is swallowed up in love. The fear that remains is the fear of causing him grief in his love for us.

(7) Love of God and love of other people are indissolubly connected (verses 7, 11, 20–1). As C. H. Dodd admirably puts it, 'The energy of love discharges itself along lines

which form a triangle, whose points are God, self, and neighbour.' If God loves us, we are bound to love each other, because it is our destiny to reproduce the life of God in humanity and the life of eternity in time. John says, with almost crude bluntness, that anyone who claims to love God and hates a brother or sister is nothing but a liar. The only way to prove that we love God is to love the men and women whom God loves. The only way to prove that God is within our hearts is constantly to show the love for others within our lives.

In this passage, there occurs what is probably the greatest single statement about God in the whole Bible, that *God is love*. It is amazing how many doors that single statement unlocks and how many questions it answers.

(1) It is the explanation of *creation*. Sometimes we are bound to wonder why God created this world. The disobedience and the lack of response in human beings is a continual grief to him. Why should he create a world which was to bring him nothing but trouble? The answer is that creation was essential to his very nature. If God is love, he cannot exist in lonely isolation. Love must have someone to love and someone to love it.

(2) It is the explanation of *free will*. Unless love is a free response, it is not love. Had God been only law, he could have created a world in which people moved like robots, having no more choice than a machine. But, if God had made people like that, there would have been no possibility of a personal relationship between him and them. Love is of necessity the free response of the heart; and, therefore, God, by a deliberate act of self-limitation, had to endow men and women with free will.

(3) It is the explanation of *providence*. Had God been simply mind and order and law, he might, so to speak, have created the universe, wound it up, set it going and left it. There are gadgets and pieces of equipment which we are urged to buy because we can install them and forget them; their most attractive quality is that they can be left to run themselves. But, because God is love, his creating act is followed by his constant care.

(4) It is the explanation of *redemption*. If God had been only law and justice, he would simply have left men and women to the consequences of their sin. The moral law would operate; the soul that sinned would die; and the eternal justice would inexorably hand out its punishments. But the very fact that God is love meant that he had to seek out and to save the lost. He had to find a remedy for sin.

(5) It is the explanation of the *life beyond*. If God were simply creator, human beings might live their brief span and die forever. The life which ended early would be only another flower which the frost of death had withered too soon. But the fact that God is love makes it certain that the chances and changes of life do not have the last word and that his love will readjust the balance of this life.

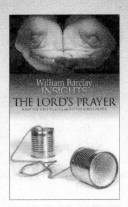

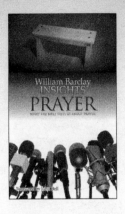

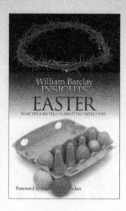

Easter

What the Bible Tells Us about the Easter Story

WILLIAM BARCLAY

Foreword by
DIANE LOUISE JORDAN

978-0-7152-0860-1 (paperback)

See our website for details.

www.standrewpress.com

SAINT ANDREW PRESS

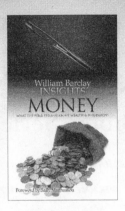

  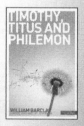

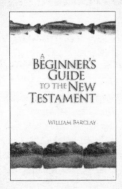

Books by
WILLIAM BARCLAY

INSIGHTS SERIES

The Lord's Prayer
Christmas
Easter
Money
Prayer
Joy
Parables
Miracles
Forgiveness
Love

THE NEW DAILY STUDY BIBLE

The Gospel of Matthew Vol. 1
The Gospel of Matthew Vol. 2
The Gospel of Mark
The Gospel of Luke
The Gospel of John Vol. 1
The Gospel of John Vol. 2
The Acts of the Apostles
The Letter to the Romans
The Letters to the Corinthians
The Letters to the Galatians and the Ephesians
The Letters to the Philippians, Colossians and Thessalonians
The Letters to Timothy, Titus and Philemon
The Letter to the Hebrews
The Letters to James and Peter
The Letters of John and Jude
The Revelation of John Vol. 1
The Revelation of John Vol. 2

MISCELLANEOUS

A Beginner's Guide to the New Testament
God's Young Church